Macronutrients & Micronutrients
A Beginners Guide to Nutrition

Contents

Chapter 1
Introduction to Nutrition

Nutrients are the essential substances found in food that provide the energy and raw materials necessary for the proper functioning of the body. These include carbohydrates, proteins, fats, vitamins, minerals and water. The primary goal of nutrition is to ensure that you receive the right balance of nutrients to support growth, development and overall well-being. A well rounded and adequate diet is crucial for the maintenance of optimal health, as different nutrients play specific roles in various physiological functions. Nutrition also addresses the concept of dietary patterns and their impact on health. Different populations may have distinct dietary habits influenced by cultural, economics and environmental factors. Understanding nutrition involves not only examining individual nutrients but also considering the overall composition of diets and their potential effects on preventing or causing various health conditions.

A balanced diet ensures that the body receives a diverse array of essential nutrients in the right proportions, therefore promoting optimal functioning and development. A balanced diet can provide the necessary energy for daily activities and helps regulate metabolic functions. Carbohydrates are the primary source of energy, while proteins play a vital role in tissue repair and growth. Fats are essential for cell structure and function and vitamins and minerals act as catalysts in numerous biochemical reactions. We will look into these in greater detail later on in the book.

A balanced diet is instrumental in preventing malnutrition and associated health issues. Adequate intake of vitamins and minerals supports the immune system, protecting the body against infections and diseases. Proper nutrition is pivotal in maintaining a healthy weight, reducing the risk of chronic conditions such as obesity, diabetes and cardiovascular diseases.

For different stages in life, from infancy to old age, a balanced diet is crucial for growth, development and maintenance of optimal health. In children, it supports physical and cognitive growth, while in adults it helps sustain energy levels and overall vitality. A balanced diet contributes to mental well-being, influencing mood and cognitive function. The importance of a balanced diet lies in its role as a foundation for good health. It not only provides the necessary nutrients for daily function but also serves as a preventive measure against a number of health challenges, contributing to a long and healthy life.

Chapter 2
Macronutrients: The Building Blocks

In this chapter we will look at the fundamental components that fuel our bodies and sustain life: carbohydrates, proteins and fats. We will delve into the intricacies of their roles, sources and recommended daily intakes.

Starting with carbohydrates, the primary energy source for the body, we will unravel the distinctions between simple and complex carbohydrates, uncovering their diverse functions, sources and the guidelines that govern their optimal consumption. We will then move on to proteins, explaining the complexity of amino acids, protein synthesis and the ongoing debate between animal and plant-based protein sources. We also shed light on the recommended daily intake for maintaining a well-nourished body. Then onto fats, that are often misunderstood. We will explore the different types of fats - saturated, unsaturated and trans fats, whilst unveiling their crucial role in bodily functions. Understanding the importance of balanced fat intake is key to unlocking the full potential of a healthy lifestyle.

Throughout this chapter, the aim is to empower you with knowledge, enabling you to make informed choices that contribute to your overall health and well-being.

Carbohydrates

Carbohydrates are one of the essential macronutrients and serve as a primary source of energy in the human body. They come in various forms, including simple and complex carbohydrates, each playing distinct roles in cellular metabolism and biological functions. Carbohydrates are integral to numerous physiological processes, such as energy storage, transport and structural support, making them fundamental to the human body.

Simple Carbohydrates

Simple carbohydrates, also known as sugars, play crucial roles in providing quick and easily accessible energy for the body. The primary function of simple carbohydrates is to serve as a rapid source of glucose, which is a key fuel for cellular activities. Upon consumption, these sugars are swiftly broken down into glucose, allowing for a prompt increase in blood sugar levels, providing immediate energy for metabolic processes.

In addition to their energy providing functions, simple carbohydrates also contribute to the sweetness and palatability of many foods, influencing taste preferences and dietary choices. Some carbohydrates, such as those found in fruits, also contain essential vitamins, minerals and fibre, contributing to overall nutritional well-being.

Sources:
Fruits: Natural sugars like fructose are found in various fruits such as apples, oranges and berries.
Honey: A natural sweetener produced by bees, honey contains a combination of fructose and glucose.
Table Sugar (Sucrose): Commonly derived from sugar cane or sugar beets, sucrose is a disaccharide ('double sugar') composed of glucose and fructose.

Milk: Lactose, a disaccharide found in milk, is broken down into glucose and galactose during digestion.
Sweets (Candy): Many processed foods, desserts and sweets contain added sugars like sucrose, glucose and fructose.

While simple carbohydrates offer quick energy, it is essential to consume them in moderation as excessive intake can lead to rapid spikes and crashes in blood sugar levels. The recommended daily intake of simple carbohydrates can vary based on factors such as age, sex, physical activity levels and overall health. General guidelines provided by health organisations suggest that added sugars, including those from simple carbohydrates, should account for no more than 10% of our total daily calorie intake.

For adults consuming a standard 2,000 calorie diet this would mean limiting added sugars to about 200 calories per day, which is equivalent to approximately 50 grams or 12 teaspoons. It is important to note that this limit is for added sugars and does not include naturally occurring sugars found in foods like fruit and dairy products.

These recommendations align with guidelines from organisations such as the World Health Organisation (WHO). However it is crucial to consider individual health conditions and goals. Those with specific health concerns, such as diabetes or obesity, may benefit from further reducing their intake of simple carbohydrates. Always consult with a healthcare professional or a registered dietitian for personalised advice based on individual needs and health status.

Complex Carbohydrates

Complex carbohydrates serve as a valuable source of sustained energy due to their more intricate molecular structure. The digestive process breaks down complex carbohydrates into simple sugars, primarily glucose, as a slower rate compared to simple carbohydrates. This gradual release of glucose helps maintain stable blood sugar levels and provides a steady and prolonged source of energy for the body.

Complex carbohydrates often accompany dietary fibre, which plays a crucial role in promoting digestive health. Fibre adds bulk to the diet, aiding in the prevention of constipation and contributing to a feeling of fullness, which can be beneficial for weight management. Certain complex carbohydrates, such as starches, serve as a storage form of energy and are vital for human nutrition.

Sources:
Whole Grains: Foods like brown rice, quinoa, oats and whole wheat products are rich in complex carbohydrates, providing sustained energy along with essential nutrients like fibre, vitamins and minerals.
Legumes: Beans, lentils and peas are excellent sources of complex carbohydrates, offering a combination of fibre and protein for a well-rounded nutritional profile.
Vegetables: Many vegetables including sweet potatoes, corn and carrots contain complex carbohydrates, vitamins and fibre.
Fruits: While fruits primarily contain simple carbohydrates, some fruits like bananas and apples also provide a moderate amount of complex carbohydrates along with

fibre and other nutrients.

Tubers and Roots: Foods like potatoes and yams are starchy vegetables that contribute significant amounts of complex carbohydrates to the diet.

Incorporating a variety of complex carbohydrates into your diet is recommended for promoting overall health, providing sustained energy and supporting proper digestive function. There isn't a specific recommended daily intake for complex carbohydrates as a separate category because dietary recommendations usually focus on overall carbohydrate intake, including both simple and complex. However general dietary guidelines provides a recommended range for total carbohydrate intake as a percentage of total daily calories.

According to the WHO, carbohydrates should make up about 45-65% of daily calorie intake. The exact proportion within this range can vary based on individual factors such as age, sex, activity level and overall health.

It is important to note that the emphasis is often on choosing healthier sources of carbohydrates, such as complex carbohydrates found in whole grains, legumes, vegetables and fruits.

For personalised dietary recommendations, you are encouraged to consult with healthcare professionals or registered dietitians. These experts can consider individual needs, preferences and goals to provide specific guidance on the ideal distribution of carbohydrates in your diet.

Protein

Proteins are crucial biomolecules that play essential roles in the structure and function of the human body. Compromising of amino acids, proteins are a fundamental component of the human diet and serve as one of the three primary macronutrients. Proteins contribute significantly to various physiological functions including tissue repair, immune response.

Proteins provide a source of energy but their primary importance lies in their role as building blocks for tissues and organs. Amino acids, the smaller units that make up proteins, are vital for the synthesis and maintenance of muscles, enzymes, hormones and other critical molecules in the body. Striking the right balance of macronutrients, including an adequate intake of proteins, is essential for supporting overall health and well-being.

Amino Acids

Amino acids are the essential components that make up proteins.
Their functions include:

Building and Repair: Amino acids are used for building and repairing tissues. They play a crucial role in the growth and maintenance of different parts of your body.
Enzymes and Chemical Reactions: Some amino acids act as catalysts, facilitating chemical reactions. Enzymes, made from amino acids, accelerate processes in your body.

Transport and Communication: Amino acids are involved in carrying messages and transporting substances within your body. They function as messengers and carriers.

Sources
Meat and Fish: Foods like chicken, beef and fish are rich sources of amino acids, providing a diverse range for various bodily functions.

Dairy Products: Milk, cheese and yoghurt contribute amino acids, offering a variety of building blocks for protein synthesis (see below).

Beans and Legumes: Lentils, chickpeas and black beans provide different types of amino acids, supporting overall protein diversity.

Nuts and Seeds: Almonds, peanuts and sunflower seeds offer specific amino acids, contributing to the pool of building blocks for proteins.

Eggs: Eggs are a versatile source of amino acids, supplying a range of components necessary for protein synthesis.

Protein Synthesis

Imagine your body is like a factory that makes proteins, which are like the workers doing an important job, here is how it works:

1. Master Plan (DNA):
Inside your body, there is a master plan called DNA. It is like the boss giving instructions on how to make different proteins.

2. Copy the Instructions (mRNA): To build the proteins, we need a copy of the boss's instructions. This copy is called mRNA and it is like a travel sized guidebook.

3. Construction Workers (Ribosome): Now we have these workers called Ribosome. They read the guidebook (mRNA) and start putting together the proteins, step by step.

4. Building the Protein: The Ribosome use amino acids, which are like building blocks and follow the guidebook's instructions to create the protein. It is like building a specific toy with different pieces.

5. The Finished Product: When the protein is complete, it goes off to do its job within your body. It is like releasing the finished toys to perform different tasks.

Protein synthesis is like following a set of instructions to build important workers (proteins) that help run your body smoothly!

Animal Protein vs Plant-Based Protein

The debate around animal-based and plant-based proteins is complex, with considerations spanning health, environment, ethics and accessibility. We are going to look into the health considerations and functions in our bodies as well as the dietary diversity and accessibility between animal and plant-based proteins.

Animal Based Proteins

Animal proteins are rich in essential amino acids, particularly those crucial for building and repairing muscles. This makes them effective for supporting muscle growth and maintenance. Animal sources often provide complete proteins thatcontain all essential amino acids in the right proportions. This wholeness is beneficial for various bodily functions. They are also an excellent source of vitamin B12 and heme iron, both important for energy production and preventing anaemia.

As stated, animal proteins are rich in complete proteins, certain vitamins and minerals essential for muscle development and overall health. The down side of animal proteins is that they come with saturated fats and cholesterol, which may be a concern for cardiovascular health when consumed excessively.

Sources:
Meat: Beef, poultry, fish and other animal meats.
Dairy: Milk, cheese, yoghurt and eggs.

Animal proteins are often widely available and accessible in various regions, contributing to their widespread inclusion in diets. In many cultures, animal based proteins play a significant role in traditional cuisines and dietary practices.

Plant Based Proteins

Plant based proteins when part of a balanced diet may contribute to heart health by offering fibre, antioxidants and healthy fats. They often come with dietary fibre, aiding digestion and promoting a healthy gut microbe. A diet rich in plant based proteins has been associated with a lower risk of certain chronic diseases including heart disease and some types of cancer. Plant based proteins may lack certain amino acids and therefore, some individuals might need to combine different plant sources or take a supplement to ensure a complete essential amino acid profile.

Sources:
Legumes: Lentils, chickpeas and beans.
Nuts and Seeds: Almonds, peanuts, chia seeds and hemp seeds.
Grains: Quinoa, brown rice and whole wheat products.
Vegetables: Broccoli, spinach and peas.

The accessibility of plant based proteins can vary depending on location and local agriculture. In some regions a variety of plant foods may be readily available, while in others options might be limited. While plant based diets are gaining popularity they may not align with certain cultural or regional food traditions, making it challenging for some individuals to adopt these dietary patterns.

A balanced diet that includes a variety of protein sources, whether from animals or plants, can contribute to overall health. Individual nutritional needs and preferences should guide the choice between animal and plant based proteins. The recommended daily intake of protein can vary based on factors such as age, sex, activity level and individual health goals. However, general dietary guidelines provide a range for protein intake expressed as a percentage of total daily calorie intake.

According to the WHO protein should typically contribute to about 10-35% of total caloric intake. For a standard adult diet based on a 2,000 calorie per day intake, this would equate for approximately 50 to 175 grams of protein per day within that range.

It is important to note that individual protein needs may differ. Athletes, pregnant people and those with specific health conditions may require higher protein intake. On the other hand, individuals with certain kidney conditions may need to monitor their protein intake and specific dietary recommendations should be tailored based on individual health needs.

For personalised advice on protein intake, it is recommended to consult with healthcare professionals or registered dietitians who can take into account individual factors and provide guidance based on specific needs and goals.

Fats

Fats are organic compounds crucial for various physiological function within the human body. Composed of carbon, hydrogen and oxygen atoms, fats serve as an essential energy reserve, insulation and structural component for cells. Their unique molecular structures, characterised by long hydrocarbon chains, distinguishes them from other macronutrients. Fats play integral roles in nutrient absorption, hormone synthesis and the maintenance of cellular membranes. The diversity of fats, ranging from saturated to unsaturated forms contributes to their varied functions in supporting overall health and well-being.

Types of Fats

Saturated Fats:
Saturated fats provide a concentrated source of energy and contribute to the structural integrity of cell membranes. However, excessive intake may be associated with an increased risk of cardiovascular disease.
Sources:
Found in animal products like meat, poultry, dairy (butter, cheese) as well as tropical oils (coconut oil, palm oil).

Unsaturated Fats:
Unsaturated fats, including mono-unsaturated and polyunsaturated fats, support heart health by helping to lower bad cholesterol levels. They also play a role in nutrient absorption and hormone production.
Sources:
Mono-unsaturated fats are found in olive oil, avocados and nuts. Polyunsaturated fats include omega-3 and omega-6 fatty acids, present in fatty fish (salmon, mackerel), flaxseed, chia seeds and walnuts.

Trans Fats:
Artificial trans fats, often created through hydrogenation, can contribute to an increased risk of cardiovascular diseases and are best avoided. In some animal products, trans fats can be found in small amounts.
Sources:
Partially hydrogenated oils in certain processed foods like fried snacks, baked goods and margarine.

Omega-3 Fatty Acids:
Omega-3s are crucial for brain health, reducing

inflammation and supporting cardiovascular function. They play a role in preventing chronic diseases.
Sources: Fatty fish (salmon, mackerel, sardines), flaxseed, chia seeds, walnuts and certain algae-based supplements.

Omega-6 Fatty Acids:
Omega-6s are essential for growth and development but an imbalance with omega-3s may contribute to inflammation. A proper ratio is essential for overall health. While there is no agreed-upon ratio, many health experts suggest aiming for a balanced or slightly higher intake of omega-3 fatty acids compared to omega-6 fatty acids (1:1 to 4:1).
Sources: Vegetable oils (soy bean oil, corn oil, sunflower oil), nuts, seeds and certain grains.

Dietary Cholesterol:
Dietary cholesterol, found exclusively in animal products, is a substance for synthesising hormones and vitamin D.
Sources: Egg yolks, organ meats (heart, liver) and high-fat dairy products.

Fats plays a crucial role in the body, serving as essential components that contribute to various physiological functions.
Here is an overall explanation of the roles of fats in the body:

Energy Source: Fats are a concentrated and efficient energy source. When the body needs energy, it breaks down fats into fatty acids, which can then be utilised for fuel. This is especially important during prolonged physical activity or times of low food intake.

Cellular Structure: Fats are integral components of cell membranes. Phospholipids, a type of fat, help maintain the structure and integrity of cell membranes, influencing cellular function and communication.

Nutrient Absorption: Fats play a crucial role in the absorption of fat-soluble vitamins (A, D, E and K) in the digestive system. (We will look into vitamins in chapter 4).

Insulation and Temperature Regulation: Adipose tissue, commonly known as body fat, acts as insulation, helping to regulate body temperature. It provides a cushioning effect, protecting organs and tissues.

Hormone Production: Fats are involved in the synthesis of hormones, including sex hormones (oestrogen and testosterone) and certain signalling molecules. Hormones regulate various physiological processes, including growth, metabolism and reproductive functions.

Brain Health: The brain contains a significant amount of fat and certain fats, particularly omega-3 fatty acids, are crucial for cognitive function, memory and overall brain health.

Inflammation Regulation: Fats influence the body's inflammation response. While some fats may contribute to inflammation, others like omega-3 fatty acids, have anti-inflammatory properties.

Satiation and Satiety: Fats contribute to the feeling of fullness and satisfaction after a meal. Including healthy fats in the diet can help control appetite and support weight management.

It is important to note that not all fats are the same and the type of fats consumed matter for overall health. Dietary recommendations for fat intake can vary based on factors such as age, sex, activity level and overall health. However, general guidelines provided by the WHO suggest that fats should constitute 20-35% of total daily caloric intake.

Saturated fats should typically make up less than 10% of daily calorie intake. This is to help reduce the risk of cardiovascular diseases. The intake of trans fats should be kept as low as possible. Many health organisations recommend minimising or eliminating the consumption of trans fats due to their association with an increased risk of heart disease. The majority of fat intake should come from unsaturated fats. This includes both mono-unsaturated and polyunsaturated fats. These fats can be beneficial for heart health.

It is important to note that while dietary fats are an essential part of a balanced diet, the emphasis should be on choosing healthy sources of fat, such as those found in nuts, seeds, avocados and fatty fish, while limiting the intake of unsaturated and trans fats often found in processed and fried foods.

For personalised dietary advice, individuals are encouraged to consult with healthcare professionals or registered dietitians. These experts can consider individual health needs, preferences and goals to provide specific guidelines on fat intake as part of an overall healthy eating plan.

Chapter 3
Overlooked Nutrients

This chapter explores two elements often overlooked in the realm of nutrition: alcohol and water. While alcohol is not traditionally classified as a macronutrient, its presence and impact on the body's metabolism are significant. Delving into the definition and metabolism of alcohol this section uncovers its unique role in nutrition, shedding light on its effects on overall health.

Water is often overlooked as a nutrient, but plays a pivotal role in maintaining physiological balance and sustaining life. Examining the importance and diverse functions of water within the body this chapter emphasises the often underestimated significance of proper hydration in supporting optimal health and well-being.

Alcohol

While alcohol does contribute calories, it is considered a separate category from macronutrients due to its distinct properties, effects on the body and non-essential nature. Alcohol does not serve as a primary source of nutrients required for bodily functions and it lacks the structural and metabolic roles fulfilled by carbohydrates, proteins and fats.

Alcohol is a psychoactive substance classified as a depressant that affects the nervous system. Its consumption results in various physiological and psychological effects, influencing mood, cognition and behaviour. Ethanol is the primary form of alcohol found in drinks and its consumption has been intertwined with culture, social and recreational practices throughout human history.

When alcohol (ethanol) is consumed, its metabolism primary takes place in the liver. The process involves several steps:

1. Absorption:
After ingestion, alcohol is rapidly absorbed into the bloodstream through the stomach and small intestine.
2. Distribution:
Once in the bloodstream, alcohol is distributed throughout the body, affecting various organs and tissues.
3. Liver Metabolism:
The liver plays a central role in metabolising alcohol. Enzymes break down alcohol into acetaldehyde, a toxic substance.
4. Acetaldehyde to Acetate:
Acetaldehyde is further metabolised into acetate, a less harmful substance, by another set of enzymes.
5. Acetate to Carbon Dioxide and Water:
Acetate is eventually converted into carbon dioxide and water, which can be easily eliminated from the body.

During this process, the liver prioritises alcohol metabolism over other metabolic processes, potentially affecting the breakdown of nutrients, including fats and carbohydrates.

Effects of Alcohol on Nutrition

While contributing to overall caloric intake, alcohol poses

unique challenges to nutrition as it lacks essential nutrients and can potentially lead to deficiencies within the body. Alcohol can interfere with nutrient absorption, impair macronutrient metabolism and influence dietary choices, impacting overall health.

Let's look into this in more detail.

Calorie Contribution:
Alcohol provides around 7 calories per gram, contributing to overall energy intake. However these calories lack essential nutrients, which is often referred to "empty calories".

Nutrient Absorption:
Alcohol can interfere with the absorption of certain nutrients in the digestive tract, including vitamins and minerals. Chronic alcohol consumption may lead to nutrient deficiencies.

Impaired Macronutrient Metabolism:
The metabolism of fats, proteins and carbohydrates may be affected by alcohol consumption, particularly when the liver prioritises alcohol metabolism.

Appetite and Dietary Choices:
Alcohol can influence appetite and food choices. Some individuals may consume more calories and make less healthy food choices when under the influence of alcohol.

Dehydration and Electrolyte Imbalance:
Alcohol is a diuretic, meaning it increases urine production, potentially leading to dehydration. This

coupled with impaired electrolyte balance can impact overall hydration status.

Liver Function:
Excessive alcohol consumption can lead to liver damage, affecting its ability to metabolise nutrients and perform essential functions. This can contribute to malnutrition over time.

Weight Management:
Regular and excessive alcohol consumption is associated with weight gain, as alcoholic drinks contribute additional calories to the diet.

There isn't a universally recommended daily intake of alcohol applicable to everyone, as individual tolerance and health considerations vary. However health organisations such as the Centre for Disease Control and Prevention (CDC) provide general guidelines for moderate alcohol consumption. Moderate drinking is often defined as not regularly drinking more than 3 to 4 units of alcohol per day for men and 2 to 3 units of alcohol per day for women.

These guidelines are based on the concept of 'units' which represent the amount of pure alcohol in a drink. In the UK one unit is equivalent to 10 millilitres (or 8 grams) of pure alcohol. Examples of one unit include approximately a singly small shot (25ml) of spirits with 40% alcohol content, half a pint of a normal strength beer or a small glass (125ml) of wine with about 12% alcohol content.

It is important to note that these guidelines are general recommendations and individual health concerns, medications and personal circumstances should be considered. It is crucial to approach alcohol consumption in moderation, taking into consideration its potential impact on overall nutrition and health. For those with specific health conditions or concerns, consulting with healthcare professionals or registered dietitians is advised to ensure a balanced and healthy lifestyle.

Water

Within the human body and nutrition, water is an unsung hero. Beyond being a simple drink, it plays a crucial role in keeping our bodies functioning properly. Every cell, tissue and organ relies on water to carry out essential tasks. From aiding digestion and nutrient absorption to regulating body temperature, water is an indispensable partner in maintaining overall health. Its significance spans various physiological functions, contributing to the overall balance and vitality of our biology systems.

Here are key aspects highlighting the importance of water:

Hydration and Cellular Function:
Water is a fundamental element for maintaining the balance of fluids within and around cells. Proper hydration ensures optimal cellular function, supporting biochemical reactions necessary for life.

Temperature Regulations:
Through processes like sweating and respiration the body releases heat to regulate its temperature. Water plays a crucial role in these mechanisms, helping to cool the body and prevent overheating.

Nutrient Transportation:
Water serves as a carrier for essential nutrients, transporting them to cells and tissues. This facilitates the absorption of nutrients from the digestive system into the bloodstream, where they can be utilised by the body.

Joint Lubrication:
Water is a key component of synovial fluid, which lubricates joints and reduces friction between bones. This is essential for smooth joint movements and flexibility.

Digestion and Metabolism:
Adequate water intake supports the digestive process, helping break down food and absorb nutrients. It also contributes to metabolic reaction, ensuring the efficient conversion of nutrients into energy.

Waste Removal:
Water plays a vital role in the elimination of waste products from the body. It supports kidney function, helping filter and excrete waste through urine. Proper hydration is essential for preventing kidney stones and maintaining urinary tract health.

Maintaining Blood Volume and Pressure:
Water is a major component of blood, contributing to its volume and aiding in the regulation of blood pressure. Maintaining adequate hydration supports cardiovascular health.

Cognitive Function:
Dehydration can impair cognitive function, affecting

concentration, alertness and overall mental performance. Proper hydration is crucial for optimal brain function.

In this next section we will look into the signs the body exhibits when it is not getting enough water and the recommended daily intake. Understanding these are essential to maintaining optimal health.

Signs of Dehydration:

Thirst: Feeling thirsty is one of the initial signals that the body needs more water. It serves as a natural mechanism to prompt fluid intake.

Dark Urine: Dark yellow or amber coloured urine can be an indicator of dehydration. Adequately hydrated individuals typically have lighter coloured urine.

Infrequent Urination: Reduced frequency of urination or passing small amounts of concentrated urine can indicate dehydration.

Dry Mouth and Sticky Saliva: Insufficient water intake can lead to reduced saliva production, resulting in a dry or sticky feeling in the mouth.

Fatigue and Lethargy: Dehydration may cause a decrease in energy levels, leading to feelings of fatigue and lethargy.

Headaches: Lack of proper hydration can contribute to headaches and migraines. Staying hydrated supports optimal blood flow to the brain.

Dizziness or Light-headedness: Dehydration may lead to a drop in blood pressure, causing dizziness or light-headedness.

Dry Skin and Eyes: Inadequate water levels can result in dry skin and eyes as the body prioritises water for vital functions.

Muscle Cramps: Dehydration may contribute to muscle cramps and spasms due to an imbalance in electrolytes.

While individual water needs can vary based on factors such as age, activity level, climate and health status, general guidelines provide a foundation for maintaining hydration. The UK National Health Service (NHS) suggest a daily fluid intake recommendation that includes water obtained from beverages and food.

The general guidelines for adults is to drink about 6-8 glasses (roughly 1.2 - 1.9 litres) of fluid per day from liquids such as water, lower fat milk and sugar free drinks. Water content from foods such as watermelon, cucumber, oranges and berries, as well as other beverages such as tea, decaffeinated coffee and coconut water contribute to meeting overall hydration needs.

It is crucial to be mindful of added sugars in certain beverages, as excessive sugar intake can have adverse health effects. Water remains the healthiest and most accessible choice for hydration.

Chapter 4
Micronutrients: The Essential Nutrients in Small Quantities

Micronutrients play an important role in the body, representing the essential elements we require in relatively small quantities. Vitamins and minerals stand as fundamental contributors to overall health and well-being. In this chapter we will unravel the complexities of vitamins and minerals, exploring their diverse roles within our body.

The initial focus on vitamins, both water-soluble and fat soluble, looking at their distinct characteristics and functions within the body. From understanding the delicate balance of recommended daily intake to exploring the unique contribution of each vitamin, this section will provide a comprehensive look into the world of these essential micronutrients.

Following the exploration of vitamins, we will look into minerals, categorised as major and trace minerals. We will help you understand the significance of minerals in maintaining optimal health, illuminating their roles in various physiological processes.
The aim is to help you understand the nuances of these essential components, providing a solid foundation for your overall health and well-being.

Micronutrients are essential elements that the human body require in relatively small quantities to maintain proper physiological function, growth and overall health. While they may be needed in smaller amounts compared to macronutrients, micronutrients play crucial roles in numerous biochemical processes that are vital for sustaining life. Micronutrients primarily include vitamins and minerals, each with specific functions within the body.

Vitamins

Vitamins are organic compounds that are essential for various physiological functions in the human body. Unlike macronutrients, vitamins are required in smaller amounts but are equally vital for maintaining proper bodily function.

Water-Soluble Vitamins

Water-soluble vitamins are a group of organic compounds that dissolve in water. Water-soluble vitamins are not stored in significant amounts and any excess is usually excreted through urine. As a result, regular intake of water-soluble vitamins is essential to meet the body's requirements. The major water-soluble vitamins include vitamin C and the B-complex vitamins.

Vitamin C (Ascorbic Acid):
Vitamin C is known for its antioxidant properties, helping to protect cells from oxidative damage. It is also essential for collagen synthesis, wound healing and the absorption of non-heme iron (found in plan-based foods).
Sources:
Found if citrus fruits (oranges, lemons), strawberries, kiwi, bell peppers, broccoli and other fruits and vegetables.

B-Complex Vitamins:
B1 (Thiamine):
Essential for energy metabolism and nerve function.
Sources:
Found in whole grains, legumes, pork and seeds.

B2 (Riboflavin):
Involved in energy production, cellular growth and the metabolism of fats, drugs and steroids.
Sources:
Found in dairy products, lean meats, green leafy vegetables and almonds.

B3 (Niacin):
Plays a role in energy metabolism and DNA repair.
Sources:
Found in meat, poultry, fish, whole grains and legumes.

B6 (Pyridoxine):
Essential for amino acid metabolism, neurotransmitter synthesis and haemoglobin formation.
Sources:
Found in meat, fish, poultry, bananas and potatoes.

B12 (Cobalamin):
Important for red blood cell formation, DNA synthesis and nerve function.
Sources:
Found in animal products such as meat, fish, eggs and dairy.

These water-soluble vitamins are critical for maintaining overall health and a well-balanced diet that includes a variety of foods to ensure an adequate intake of those essential nutrients. While cooking methods can affect the vitamin content in foods, consuming a diverse range of nutrient-rich foods is key to meeting the body's water-soluble vitamin needs.

The recommended daily intake of water-soluble vitamins varies depending on factors such as age, sex and individual health needs. Generally, the recommended dietary allowance (RDA) serves as a guideline. For instance, the RDA for vitamin C ranges from 75 to 90 milligrams per day for most adults. B-complex vitamins have a specific RDA, for example, for vitamin B12 2.4 micrograms is recommended for adults. As these vitamins are not stored in the body for extended periods, consistent daily intake through a balanced diet is essential.

Fat-Soluble Vitamins

Fat-soluble vitamins are a group of organic compounds that dissolve in fats and are absorbed along with dietary fat in the small intestine. Unlike water-soluble vitamins, fat-soluble can be stored in the body's fatty tissues and liver, allowing for a reserve that can be utilised when dietary intake is insufficient. The major fat-soluble vitamins include vitamins A, D, E and K.

Vitamin A (Retinol, Retinal, Retinoic Acid):
Essential for vision, immune function, skin health and proper functioning of organs such as the heart and lungs.
Sources:
Found in liver, fish oil, dairy products, eggs and orange and dark vegetables.

Vitamin D (Calciferol):
Crucial for calcium absorption and bone health. Also plays a role in immune function.
Sources:
Synthesized by the skin in response to sunlight (UVB rays). Dietary sources include fatty fish (salmon, mackerel), fish liver oils, egg yolks and fortified dairy products.

Vitamin E (Tocopherols, Tocotrienols):
Acts as an antioxidant, protecting cells from oxidative damage. Supports immune function and skin health.
Sources:
Found in nuts, seeds, vegetable oils (such as sunflower and wheat germ oil), spinach and broccoli.

Vitamin K (Phylloquinone, Menquinone):
Necessary for blood clotting, bone metabolism and cell growth regulation.
Sources:
Found in green leafy vegetables (such as kale, spinach), broccoli, Brussels sprouts and certain oils.

Maintaining an adequate intake of fat-soluble vitamins is important for overall health, but excessive amounts can lead to toxicity due to their storage in the body. Consuming a varied and balanced diet that includes a mix of nutrient-rich foods ensures a proper supply of these essential fat-soluble vitamins. Dietary fats are crucial for the absorption of fat-soluble vitamins, emphasising the importance of a balanced approach to nutrient intake.

The recommended daily intake of fat-soluble vitamins also vary based on age, sex and individual health considerations. These vitamins have adequate intake (AI) levels and for some, tolerable upper intake levels (UL) are established to prevent toxicity. For instance, the AI for vitamin D ranges from 400 to 800 international units (UI) for adults, depending on age, while the UL is set at 4,000 IU. Dietary sources and potential supplementation are considered in meeting these recommendations, emphasising the importance of a well-rounded and nutrient-dense diet to ensure adequate intake without the risk of excess.

Minerals

Minerals are inorganic elements necessary for various physiological processes. Common minerals include calcium, iron, zinc, magnesium and potassium. These minerals are crucial for functions like bone health, oxygen transport, enzyme activation, nerve transmission and maintaining fluid balance.

Major minerals and trace minerals are two categories of minerals that the body requires for various physiological functions, but they differ primarily in the amounts the body needs and the relative abundance in the body.

Major Minerals

Major minerals, also known as macrominerals, are minerals that the body needs in larger amounts, typically more than 100 milligrams per day. These minerals play crucial roles in maintaining proper fluid balance, nerve function and structural components of the body, such as bones and teeth. Calcium, phosphorus, magnesium, sodium, potassium, sulphur and chloride are considered major minerals. Major minerals are present in the body in significant amounts and deficiencies or imbalances can have profound effects on health.

Trace Minerals

Trace minerals are minerals that the body requires in smaller amounts, usually less than 20 milligrams per day. Although needed in smaller quantities, trace minerals are still vital for various physiological functions, including enzyme activity, immune function and the formation of certain proteins. Iron, zinc, copper, manganese, selenium, iodine and fluoride are considered trace minerals. While trace minerals are essential, they are present in the body in smaller concentrations compared to major minerals. Deficiencies can still have significant health consequences.

Importance of Minerals in Health

Minerals play a pivotal role in maintaining optimal health, influencing a wide array of functions within the human body. These essential nutrients are involved in processes ranging from bone formation and nerve transmission to enzyme activation and immune functions. Major minerals contribute to the structural integrity of bones and teeth, ensuring skeletal strength. Potassium and sodium regulate fluid balance and support nerve impulses, while iron is vital for oxygen transport in the blood. Trace minerals act as co-factors for enzymes, influencing metabolic pathways crucial for growth and immune response. Minerals like iodine are essential for thyroid hormone synthesis and fluride contributes to dental health. A well-balanced diet that includes a variety of nutrient-dense foods is crucial to ensure an adequate intake of minerals, as deficiencies or excess can lead to a range of health issues.

Chapter 5
Calories and Energy Balance

Calories serve as a fundamental unit of energy that the body derives from the food and beverages consumed. Understanding calories is essential for maintaining a healthy and balanced diet, as they represent the energy content within various macronutrients. Each gram of carbohydrate and proteins provides approximately 4 calories, while fats contribute about 9 calories per gram. By grasping these calorie values, individuals can better manage their energy intake and expenditure, supporting weight management goals.

Calorie needs vary based on factors such as age, gender, activity level and metabolic rate. Balancing calorie intake with energy expenditure is crucial for weight maintenance, loss or gain. Consuming more calories than the body burns leads to weight gain, while a calorie deficit results in weight loss. However, it is important to recognise that not all calories are equal in terms of nutritional value. Prioritising nutrient-dense foods over empty calorie options ensures that the body receives essential vitamins, minerals and other nutrients along with energy, contributing to overall health.

Calorie Expenditure

Calorie expenditure refers to the total amount of energy that an individual utilises or burns over a given period, often measured in calories or kilocalories. This expenditure includes the energy required for basic bodily functions at rest, known as the basal metabolic rate (BRM), as well as the energy used during physical activities and the thermic effect of food digestion.

The BMR accounts for the majority of calorie expenditure and represents the energy needed to sustain essential bodily functions such as maintaining body temperature, supporting organ function and repairing cells while at rest. BMR is influenced by factors like age, gender, body composition and genetics. Physical activity, another significant component of calorie expenditure, includes both planned exercise and daily activities such as walking, standing and household chores. The intensity and duration of these activities affect the overall energy expended.

The thermic effect of food (TEF) contributes to calorie expenditure and represents the energy required for digesting, absorbing and metabolising nutrients from the diet. Different macronutrients have varying thermic effects, with proteins requiring more energy for digestion compared to fats and carbohydrates. By understanding and managing calorie expenditure, individuals can make informed decisions about their dietary and exercise choices to achieve specific health and fitness goals.

Balancing Calorie Intake and Expenditure

Balancing calorie intake and expenditure is a key principle for achieving and maintaining a healthy weight. Here are several practical strategies to help you achieve this balance:

Calculate Your Basal Metabolic Rate (BMR): Determine the number of calories your body needs at rest by calculating your BMR. Numerous online calculators can provide you with an estimate based on factors such as age, gender, weight and height.

Consider Your Activity Level: Factor in your physical activity level to estimate your total daily energy expenditure (TDEE). This includes calories burned through daily activities, exercise and planned workout. Websites and apps often offer TDEE calculators to help with this estimation.

Set Realistic Goals: Establish realistic and sustainable weight related goals. Aim for a gradual, steady weight loss, gain or maintenance rather than rapid changes, which can be challenging to sustain.

Track Your Food Intake: Use a food diary or mobile apps to track your food intake. Be mindful of portion sizes and the nutritional content of the foods you consume. This awareness can help you make informed decisions about your diet.

Watch Liquid Calories: Be mindful of liquid calories from sugary beverages and alcoholic drinks. These can contribute significantly to your overall calorie intake without providing a sense of fullness.

Find a Balance that works for You: Every individual is unique and there is no one-size-fits-all approach. Experiment with different dietary patterns and exercise routines to find a balance that suits your lifestyles, preferences and health goals.

Be Consistent: Consistency is key to achieving and maintaining a balance between calorie intake and expenditure. Small, sustainable changes over time are more likely to lead to lasting results.

Remember that achieving a balance between calorie intake and expenditure is a process that may require adjustments over time. It's important to focus on overall well-being and adopt habits that contribute to a sustainable and healthy lifestyle.

Chapter 6
Digestion and Absorption

This chapter will look at the dynamic process of digestion and absorption. Journeying through the digestive system and how it breaks down our food, we will explore the absorption of nutrients, where the body extracts essential elements from the digestive environment. We will also look into the different factors that can influence affective nutrient absorption.

The Digestive System

The digestive system is a complex network of organs and processes in our body that work together to break down the food we eat into nutrients, which our body can then absorb and use for energy, growth and repair.

Imagine your digestive system as a factory that processes food. It all begins in the mouth, where you chew your food. Chewing not only makes the food smaller but also mixes it with saliva, which contains enzymes that start breaking down carbohydrates.

After chewing, the food travels down the oesophagus, a muscular tube that connects the mouth to the stomach. The food doesn't just fall straight down, muscles in the walls of the oesophagus contract in a coordinated way to push the food towards the stomach.

Once in the stomach the food is mixed with stomach acid and digestive enzymes. This creates a soupy mixture called chyme. The stomach's acidic environment helps break down proteins and kill bacteria that may be present in the food.

Next the chyme moves into the small intestine, a long tube where most of the digestion and nutrient absorption take place. The pancreas and liver release digestive enzymes and bile into the small intestine to further break down the chyme into smaller molecules that can be absorbed into the bloodstream.

The nutrients are now in a form that the body can use and are absorbed through the walls of the small intestine and bloodstream. The remaining undigested material moves into the large intestine, where water and electrolytes are absorbed, forming faeces.

Finally, the waste is stored in the rectum until it is ready to be eliminated from the body through the anus in the form of bowel movements.

The digestive system is a remarkable process that allows our bodies to extract essential nutrients from the food we eat, providing the energy and building blocks needed for our daily activities and overall health.

Absorption of Nutrients

Nutrient absorption primarily takes place in the small intestine, the longest section of the digestive tract. The small intestine is where the majority of digestion and absorption occur due to its specialised structures and processes.

Let's look into the absorption of nutrients in more detail:

Enzymatic Breakdown:
- After food leaves the stomach as chyme, it enters the first part of the small intestine, called the duodenum.
- The pancreas releases digestive enzymes into the duodenum. These enzymes break down proteins, fats and carbohydrates into smaller molecules.

Bile Action:
- The liver produces bile, which is stored in the gallbladder and released into the duodenum. Bile helps emulsify fats, breaking them into smaller droplets. This makes it easier for enzymes to access and digest fats.

Absorption in the Small Intestine:
- The lining of the small intestine has numerous finger-like structures called villi and micro-villi. These structures significantly increase the surface area for nutrient absorption.
- Nutrients, now broken down into smaller molecules (such as amino acids from proteins, fatty acids and glycerol from fats and simple sugars from carbohydrates), are absorbed through the walls of the small intestine.
- Specialised cells on the surface of the villi actively transport these nutrients across the intestinal wall and into the bloodstream.

Transportation to the Liver:
- The absorbed nutrients enter the bloodstream and are transported to the liver via the hepatic portal vein. The liver further processes and regulates the nutrient levels in the blood.

Distribution to the Body:
- The nutrient-rich blood leaving the liver is then circulated throughout the body, delivering the essential substances needed for energy, growth and various bodily functions.

It is important to note that not all nutrients are absorbed in the small intestine. For example, some water, electrolytes and certain vitamins (vitamin K, B5, B7) are absorbed in the large intestine before remaining material is formed into faeces. The efficiency of nutrient absorption is a crucial aspect of the digestive system, ensuring that our bodies receive the essential components for maintaining health and functionality.

Factors Affecting Nutrient Absorption

Nutrient absorption in the digestive system is influenced by various factors that collectively determine how efficiently the body extracts essential substances from the food we consume. One critical factor is the production of digestive enzymes. Adequate levels of these enzymes are necessary for breaking down macronutrients into smaller, easily absorbed molecules. The stomach's hydrochloric acid plays a vital role in breaking down food and activating digestive enzymes. Insufficient stomach acid can hinder the proper digestion of nutrients.

The health of the intestinal lining is another key consideration. Conditions like coeliac disease or inflammatory bowel diseases can compromise the integrity of the intestinal lining, affecting the absorption of nutrients. The surface area of the small intestine, particularly the presence of villi and micro-villi, is crucial for optimal absorption. Conditions or surgical procedures that reduce this surface area can impact efficiency.

Bile, produced by the liver and stored in the gallbladder, emulsifies fats, making them more accessible to digestive enzymes. Any issues with bile production or release can influence the absorption of fats.

Dietary factors also play a role. The presence of fibre in the diet can influence the absorption of certain minerals and consuming specific nutrients with fats can enhance the absorption of fat-soluble vitamins. Medications such as antibiotics can interfere with absorption by affecting the balance of gut bacteria.

Medical conditions like coeliac disease, Crohn's disease and pancreatic disorders can impair nutrient absorption. Individuals needs, age and overall health also contribute to the complex interplay of factors influencing nutrient absorption. If you have any concerns about your nutrients or persistent digestive issues, seeking advice from a healthcare professional is advised for a thorough assessment and appropriate guidance.

Chapter 7
Myths and Misconceptions in Nutrition

In this chapter we will unravel the myths and misconceptions that often come about in the field of nutrition. We will confront common beliefs and separate fact from fiction, aiming to shine a light on evidence-based truths. As we delve into addressing prevalent misconceptions and debunking nutritional myths, we will be guided by science, offering a reliable and informed approach to understanding the complexities of nutrition.

By shedding light on prevailing misconceptions that can influence dietary choices we aim to get rid of the confusion and empower you with accurate knowledge.

Myth: Carbohydrates are the enemy
Common belief: Carbohydrates are often vilified as the culprit behind weight gain.
Reality: There is a prevalent belief that carbohydrates are responsible for weight gain and should be limited or avoided in a healthy diet. This misconception has contributed to the popularity of various low-carbohydrate diets that suggest reducing or eliminating carbohydrate intake to promote weight loss. In reality, carbohydrates are a crucial source of energy for the body and are especially important for supporting brain function. The key to a healthy carbohydrate intake is to choose complex carbohydrates from whole grains, fruits and vegetables and limiting your consumption of simple carbohydrates (refined sugars and processed foods). Refer back to chapter 2 for more information on carbohydrates.

Myth: Protein diets are always healthy
Common belief: The more protein, the better.
Reality: Many individuals associate protein intake with muscle building, weight loss and overall well-being, leading to the idea that more protein is inherently better. Protein is indeed an essential nutrient with crucial roles in the body, including muscle development, immune function and hormone production. However, excessive protein intake can pose potential health risks. The body has a limit to how much protein it can utilise effectively and excessive intake may strain the kidneys over time. Rather than focusing solely on increasing protein intake, prioritise high-quality protein sources. Refer back to chapter 2 for more information on proteins.

Myth: Fat-free means healthy
Common belief: Choosing fat-free options guarantees a healthy diet.
Reality: Some fats are essential for health. Opting for healthy fats like those found in avocados and nuts contribute to overall well-being. Many fat-free or low-fat products undergo processing to enhance flavour and texture. This processing may involve the addition of sugars, salt or other additives, potentially compromising the overall nutritional quality of the food. Refer back to chapter 2 for more information on fats.

Myth: Skipping meals accelerates weight loss
Common belief: Skipping meals is an effective weight-loss strategy.
Reality: Skipping meals is detrimental for a number of reasons. It can slow down your metabolism, making it harder to burn calories efficiently. It can lead to low

energy levels, fatigue and reduced productivity. Skipping meals may lead to nutrient deficiencies over time, or overeating later, negatively impacting your health. Consistent, balanced meals supports sustainable weight management.

Myth: Detox diets cleanse the body
Common belief: Detox diets eliminate toxins and cleanse the body.
Reality: The widespread belief is that detox diets, often involving a specific dietary regime, fasting or the consumption of certain foods/drinks, have the ability to rid the body of accumulating toxins. Many people view these diets as a way to "reset" the body and promote overall health. In reality, the human body is equipped with sophisticated and efficient detoxification mechanisms. Organs such as the liver, kidneys, lungs and skin work together to identify, metabolise and eliminate toxins and waste products. While the intention behind detox diets is often to promote health, extreme or prolonged versions of these diets may compromise nutritional balance, leading to deficiencies in vitamins, minerals and other vital components necessary for overall well-being.

Myth: Supplements can replace a balanced diet
Common belief: Relying on supplements is sufficient for optimal nutrition.
Reality: While supplements can be valuable in filling specific nutritional gaps, they are best used as a complement to, rather than a replacement for a balanced and varied diet. Certain populations, such as those with specific deficiencies, certain medical conditions or dietary restrictions may benefit from targeted supplementation

under the guidance of a healthcare professional. Solely relying on supplements may lead to missing out on the nutritional complexity and diversity found in whole foods.

Myth: Eating late at night causes weight gain
Common belief: Consuming food late at night leads to weight gain.
Reality: Weight gain is primarily influenced by the overall balance between calorie intake and expenditure, rather than the specific time of day when you eat. The body processes and metabolises calories consistently throughout the day and night, adjusting to your regular eating patterns. Rather than fixating on the time of meals, it is more important to pay attention to the quality and quantity of the food you consume. Refer back to chapter 5 for more information on calories.

Myth: Superfoods guarantee superior health
Common belief: Superfoods possess unparalleled health benefits
Reality: Many people believe in the concept of "superfoods," thinking that certain foods have extraordinary nutritional properties that can ensure superior health. These foods are often marketed as having unique abilities to prevent disease, boost energy or provide other exceptional health benefits. In reality, while certain foods may be nutrient-dense and offer a range of health benefits, there is no single food that can guarantee overall health and well-being. Optimal health is a result of a combination of factors including a balanced and varied diet, physical activity, lifestyle choices and genetic factors.

Myth: Gluten-free equals healthier

Common belief: Gluten-free diets are inherently healthier.

Reality: For individuals diagnoses with gluten sensitivity or coeliac disease, eliminating gluten from their diet is essential for managing their conditions and preventing adverse health effects. However, for the majority of the population without gluten sensitivity, there is no inherent health benefit in adopting a gluten-free diet. In fact, gluten-containing grains such as wheat, barley and rye, are excellent sources of essential nutrients like fibre, vitamins and minerals.

Myth: Eating small, frequent meals boosts metabolism

Common belief: Grazing throughout the day accelerates metabolism.

Reality: Many people believe that eating small, frequent meals throughout the day can boost your metabolism, leading to increased calorie burning and weight loss. This idea has gained popularity and some even advocate for the concept of "grazing" or having multiple small meals to maintain a faster metabolism. In reality the impact of meal frequency on metabolism is not as significant as commonly believed. Metabolism is influenced by various factors, including genetics, age, body composition and physical activity levels. While eating does cause a temporary increase in metabolism due to the thermic effect of food, the overall effect on daily energy expenditure is relatively modest.

Science-Based Approaches to Nutrition

In the world of nutrition, balance is paramount. A healthy diet is characterised by its diversity, encompassing variety of foods to ensure a broad spectrum of nutrients. Numerous studies support the concept of balanced nutrition, emphasising the importance of a varied diet to meet the body's nutritional needs [1].

Understanding the role of macronutrients (chapter 2) is foundational. Proteins facilitate muscle repair, carbohydrates provide energy and fats serve essential function within the body. This understanding is rooted in extensive research that consistently emphasised the importance of macronutrients in maintaining health [2]. Micronutrients (chapter 3) play vital roles in various physiological functions. A diverse diet ensures an array of these essential micronutrients, each contributing to specific biochemical processes. Scientific evidence supports the notion that consuming a variety of foods is crucial for an adequate intake of micronutrients.

In the pursuit of optimal nutrition, individualised approaches take centre stage. Recognising that nutrition is not a one-size-fits-all approach and tailoring dietary choices to individuals needs, preferences and health conditions is crucial. The emerging field of nutrigenomics, which studies how individual genetic variations affect responses to nutrients, supports the idea of a personalised nutrition plan.

Distinguishing between whole foods and processed

foods is pivotal. Prioritising whole, unprocessed foods over heavily processed alternatives ensures superior nutritional values. This principle aligns with numerous studies highlighting the benefits of a diet focused on whole, minimally processed foods [3]. Hydration emerges as a fundamental component of nutrition, facilitating bodily functions, aiding digestion and supporting nutrient transport. The scientific basis for the importance of hydration is well-established, with water being essential for various physiological processes. Dehydration can negatively impact cognitive function, physical performance and overall health.

Lastly, mindfulness transforms eating habits. Paying attention to hunger and fullness cues fosters mindful eating, nurturing a healthier relationship with food. Numerous studies suggest that mindfulness can reduce overeating and emotional eating, contributing to weight management and overall well-being [4].

Remember, that when it comes to nutrition, knowledge is your greatest ally. By addressing misconceptions, debunking myths and embracing science based approaches, you equip yourself with the tools needed to navigate the often difficult topic of nutrition. Let science-based knowledge be your guide towards making choices that contribute to your overall well-being. Always consult with a healthcare professional or registered dietitian for personalised guidance based on your specific needs and health status.

Conclusion

This book has taken a comprehensive journey through the complex world of nutrition, providing you with a foundational understanding of the essential components that fuel and sustain the human body. We delved into the intricate details of macronutrients and micronutrients, focused on the often unnoticed nutrients, alcohol and water and dispelled common misconceptions in nutrition. This book aims to equip you with the knowledge needed to navigate the complex work of nutrition with more confidence.

Embarking on a journey of self-education in the realm of healthy nutrition is a commendable and empowering choice that holds the key to unlocking a world of well-being and vitality. Committing to understanding the complexity of nutrition reflects a deep-seated desire for personal growth and a healthier lifestyle. Taking the time to soak in this knowledge, remembering that learning is a gradual process and every bit of information acquired is a step towards a healthier and more informed version of yourself. Take joy in the discovery of how the foods you consume impact your body, mind and overall wellness.

Empowering yourself with knowledge is the foundation upon which healthy habits are built. Understanding the nutritional value of food, the importance of balanced meals and the impact of lifestyle choices on your health will empower you to make informed decisions that resonate with your goals and values. Remember, the knowledge you gain is a powerful tool that aids you to taking control of your health. By reading this book and educating yourself you are investing in a healthier, more nutritional future.

Glossary

Acetaldehyde: Acetaldehyde (ethanol) is an organic chemical compound that is highly reactive and toxic.

Acetate: Acetate is a human-made, semi-synthetic material derived from cellulose.

Anaemia: Is a problem of not having enough healthy red blood cells or hemoglobin to carry oxygen to the body's tissues.

Antioxidants: Antioxidants are substances that may protect your cells against free radicals, which may play a role in heart disease, cancer and other diseases. Free radicals are molecules produced when your body breaks down food or when you're exposed to tobacco smoke or radiation.

Biochemical reaction: The transformation of one molecule to a different molecule inside a cell.

Biological functions: In biology, functions are attributed to the traits, behaviours and parts of living things. A thing's function can refer to its purpose, a benefit it confers on an organism, or the causal role it contributes to a more complex system capacity.

Biomolecules: Biological molecules produced by the cells of the living organism. They are critical for life as it helps organisms to carry out basic biological processes such as reproduction, growth and sustenance.

Blood pressure: Blood pressure is the pressure of circulating blood against the walls of blood vessels. Most of this pressure results from the heart pumping blood through the circulatory system.

Blood sugar level: The blood sugar level, blood sugar concentration, blood glucose level, or glycemia, is the measure of glucose concentrated in the blood. The body tightly regulates blood glucose levels as a part of metabolic homoeostasis.

Carbon Dioxide: An important heat-trapping gas, also known as a greenhouse gas, that comes from the extraction and burning of fossil fuels (such as coal, oil, and natural gas), from wildfires, and natural processes like volcanic eruptions.

Cardiovascular diseases: The leading cause of death globally, taking an estimated 17.9 million lives each year. Cardiovascular diseases are a group of disorders of the heart and blood vessels and include coronary heart disease, cerebrovascular disease, rheumatic heart disease and other conditions.

Coeliac disease: Coeliac disease is a condition where your immune system attacks your own tissues when you eat gluten. It stops you from taking in nutrients.

Cells: Cells are the basic building blocks of all living things. The human body is composed of trillions of cells. They provide structure for the body, take in nutrients from food, convert those nutrients into energy, and carry out specialised functions.

Cellular metabolism: Cellular metabolism consists of the chemical reactions that occur in living cells. Broadly, these reactions can be divided into catabolic reactions that convert nutrients to energy and anabolic reactions that lead to the synthesis of larger biomolecules.

Cholesterol: Cholesterol is the principal sterol of all higher animals, distributed in body tissues, especially the brain and spinal cord, and in animal fats and oils.

Cognitive function: Cognitive function is a broad term that refers to mental processes involved in the acquisition of knowledge, manipulation of information, and reasoning. Cognitive functions include the domains of perception, memory, learning, attention, decision making, and language abilities.

Collagen synthesis: The process of collagen synthesis occurs mainly in the cells of fibroblasts which are specialised cells with the main function of synthesizing collagen and stroma.

Crohn's disease: Crohn's disease is a type of inflammatory bowel disease (IBD). It causes swelling of the tissues (inflammation) in your digestive tract, which can lead to abdominal pain, severe diarrhoea, fatigue, weight loss and malnutrition.

Depressant: Depressant substances reduce arousal and stimulation. They affect the central nervous system, slowing down the messages between the brain and body. They can affect concentration and coordination and slow down a person's ability to respond to unexpected situations

Diabetes: Diabetes is a chronic disease that occurs either when the pancreas does not produce enough insulin or when the body cannot effectively use the insulin it produces. Insulin is a hormone that regulates blood glucose.

DNA: The molecule that carries genetic information for the development and functioning of an organism. DNA is made of two linked strands that wind around each other to resemble a twisted ladder — a shape known as a double helix.

Enzymes: Enzymes are proteins that help speed up metabolism, or the chemical reactions in our bodies. They build some substances and break others down. All living things have enzymes. Our bodies naturally produce enzymes.

Haemoglobin: Haemoglobin is a protein found in the red blood cells that carries oxygen in your body and gives blood its red colour.

Healthcare professionals: A health professional, healthcare professional, or healthcare worker is a provider of health care treatment and advice based on formal training and experience.

Hormone synthesis: Hormones are synthesized and stored in endocrine cells and, when required, they are released into the circulatory system. A number of hormones are transported in the bloodstream by carrier proteins.

Hydrogenation: Hydrogenation turns a liquid unsaturated fat into a solid fat by adding hydrogen. Fully hydrogenated oils are mostly saturated fat and don't pose the same health risks as trans fat, so they are allowed in manufactured foods.

Immune system: The immune system is a complex network of organs, cells and proteins that defends the body against infection, whilst protecting the body's own cells. The immune system keeps a record of every germ (microbe) it has ever defeated so it can recognise and destroy the microbe quickly if it enters the body again.

Inflammation: Inflammation is an essential part of your body's healing process. It occurs when inflammatory cells travel to the place of an injury or foreign body like bacteria. If inflammatory cells stay too long, it may lead to chronic inflammation.

Inflammatory bowel diseases: Inflammatory bowel disease (IBD) is a term used to describe conditions that cause severe tummy pain and diarrhoea. IBD is long-term, but there are treatments that can help with the symptoms.

Malnutrition: Malnutrition is a serious condition that happens when your diet does not contain the right amount of nutrients. It means "poor nutrition" and can refer to: under-nutrition, not getting enough nutrients or over-nutrition, getting more nutrients than needed.

Molecular structure: The three-dimensional structure or arrangement of atoms in a molecule.

Nervous system: The nervous system includes the brain, spinal cord, and a complex network of nerves. This system sends messages back and forth between the brain and the body.

Obesity: Overweight and obesity are defined as abnormal or excessive fat accumulation that presents a risk to health.

Oestrogen: Oestrogen is one of the main female sex hormones. While both females and males produce oestrogen, it plays a bigger role in the female body. Oestrogen is part of your hormonal (endocrine) system and is mostly produced by the ovaries.

Physiological functions: Physiological functions occur when specific organs and their subsequent systems engage in specific actions. Physiological functions include a structure and a process. Structures may include single organs, whole organ systems, or even specific tissues.

Psychoactive substance: Substances that, when taken in or administered into one's system, affect mental processes, e.g. perception, consciousness, cognition or mood and emotions. Psychoactive drugs belong to a broader category of psychoactive substances that include alcohol and nicotine.

Registered dietitians: The only qualified health professionals that assess, diagnose and treat dietary and nutritional problems at an individual and wider public health level.

Testosterone: While both males and females produce testosterone, it is the main male sex hormone. Testosterone is made in the testicles for men and both the ovaries and adrenal gland for women. Testosterone hormone levels are important to a male's sexual development and functions.

Reference List

[1] National Library of Medicine (2020) 'Defining a Healthy Diet: Evidence for the Role of Contemporary Dietary Patterns in Health and Disease' Hellas Cena and Philip C. Calder.

[2]National Library of Medicine (2020) 'Macronutrients and Human Health for the 21st Century' Bernard J. Venn

[3]National Library of Medicine (2020) 'The Effects of Ultra-Processed Food Consumption - Is There Any Action Needed?' Anna Gramza-Michalowska

[4]National Library of Medicine (2014) 'Mindfulness-Based Interventions for Obesity-Related Eating Behaviours' Gillian A. O'Reilly, Lauren Cook, Donna Spruijt-Metz and David S. Black

About The Author

I am a dedicated health and well-being life coach with a passion to assist individuals in realising their full potential. My journey towards this profession has been shaped by a strong desire to make a meaningful impact on the lives of others. My understanding of the interconnected nature of holistic health and encompassing the realms of the mind, body and soul, has led me to train in life coaching, personal training and nutrition as well as holistic therapy.

My coaching methodology centres on fostering a positive and empathetic environment whilst using techniques such as visualisation, goal setting, and Neuro-Linguistic Programming (NLP).

With gratitude,

Jodie

HARMONISE HEALTH
MIND|BODY|SOUL

www.harmonisehealth.co.uk
@HarmoniseHealth

Printed in Great Britain
by Amazon

46685919R00040